W9-BRU-196

Raccoons

Julie Murray

Abdo
EVERYDAY ANIMALS
Kids

abdopublishing.com

Published by Abdo Kids, a division of ABDO, PO Box 398166, Minneapolis, Minnesota 55439.
Copyright © 2016 by Abdo Consulting Group, Inc. International copyrights reserved in all countries.
No part of this book may be reproduced in any form without written permission from the publisher.

Printed in the United States of America, North Mankato, Minnesota.

102015

012016

 THIS BOOK CONTAINS
RECYCLED MATERIALS

Photo Credits: iStock, Shutterstock

Production Contributors: Teddy Borth, Jennie Forsberg, Grace Hansen

Design Contributors: Candice Keimig, Dorothy Toth

Library of Congress Control Number: 2015941763

Cataloging-in-Publication Data

Murray, Julie.
 Raccoons / Julie Murray.
  p. cm. -- (Everyday animals)
ISBN 978-1-68080-117-0 (lib. bdg.)
Includes index.
1. Raccoons--Juvenile literature.   I. Title.
599.76--dc23
                       2015941763

Table of Contents

Raccoons

Most raccoons have gray fur.

Others have brown fur.

Their faces have black marks.

Raccoons have long tails.

Their tails have black rings.

Raccoons have sharp
claws. They have long toes.
They open doors with them.

Raccoons are active at night.

They see well in the dark.

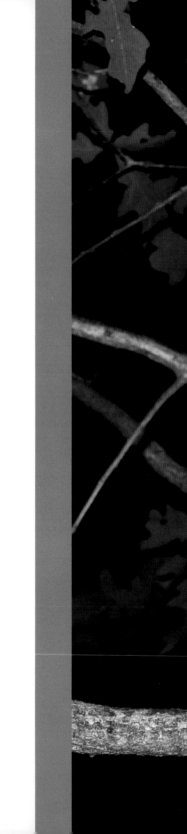

They make many sounds.

They growl and scream.

Raccoons eat many things.

They like fruit and frogs.

They even eat garbage!

They live in hollow trees and
logs. They are good climbers.

Have you seen a raccoon?

Features of a Raccoon

claws

mask

eyes

tail

Glossary

active
awake and moving.

hollow
empty inside.

mark
a spot or line on an animal's fur.

Index

abdokids.com

Use this code to log on to abdokids.com and access crafts, games, videos, and more!

Abdo Kids Code:
ERK1170

24